KELP

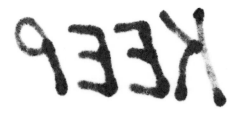

Martha and Mary

E
BAC

Published in Nashville, Tennessee, by Oliver-Nelson Books, a division of Thomas Nelson, Inc., Publishers, and distributed in Canada by Lawson Falle, Ltd., Cambridge, Ontario.

ISBN 0-8407-3418-2

Manufactured in Singapore.

1 2 3 4 5 6 7 — 97 96 95 94 93 92

Martha and Mary

Halcyon Backhouse

Illustrated by
Jenny Press

A Division of Thomas Nelson Publishers
Nashville

No one moved in the streets.
The village by the hill
was quiet.
A dog slept in the sun.
The women sewed and cooked
in the shade.

All of a sudden
there was a noise.

"Did you hear that?"
Mary asked her sister Martha.
"I am sure there was a noise.
I will find out what it was."

"Come quick," Mary said.
"It is Jesus and His friends.
There is a crowd.
Let us invite them for a meal.
You ask Him, Martha.
You are the oldest."

"Jesus!" Martha said.
"You did not tell us You were coming.
It is good to see You again.
Will you come for a meal . . .
er . . . all of you?"

Martha was thrilled.
But she was upset, too.

There was so much to do.

First she had to buy more food.

And wash it.

And cook it.

And bake bread.

And put it all out.

And pour drinks.

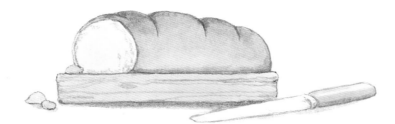

No. First she would go to the well.
She would get more water.
Jesus and His friends had to wash.
She would get lots of towels
from somewhere.

Then she would get more cups
and plates and . . .
Martha needed help.
Where was Mary?

Mary was with Jesus.
She sat on the ground with
the others.
Mary wanted to hear Jesus.

Martha felt like crying.
She said, "Jesus, do You
care about me?
I have all this work to do.
All by myself.
It is not fair.
Tell Mary she must help."

Jesus looked at Martha.

He smiled. "Oh, Martha," He said.

"You worry too much.

You put the wrong things first.

Only one thing is important.

And Mary has it right."

What do you think Martha did then?